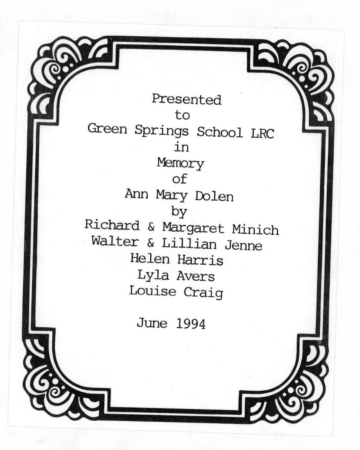

Presented
to
Green Springs School LRC
in
Memory
of
Ann Mary Dolen
by
Richard & Margaret Minich
Walter & Lillian Jenne
Helen Harris
Lyla Avers
Louise Craig

June 1994

a visit to the ZOO

Zoological Park

Summer hours

Winter hours

No Bicycle Riding

No Pets Allowed

CHILDRENS PRESS ®

CHICAGO

by Sylvia Root Tester

With special thanks to Laura Pedriani and the MILWAUKEE COUNTY ZOO, Milwaukee, Wisconsin, for assistance in the preparation of this book. While all photos do not reflect the exhibits at Milwaukee County Zoo, they are representative of what children may see and do on a visit to a major metropolitan zoo.

A thank-you also to the children from TEACHING CENTERS, Milwaukee, Wisconsin, who served as patient models.

PHOTO CREDITS

PILOT PRODUCTIONS, INC.
Dave Holmes, photographer
Jay Kelly, lighting assistant
Dean Garrison, director

Photos on cover and page 31 by Sue Markson

Photos on pages 1, 14 (top), 18 (top), 19 (right), 29 (left), and 30 (top) courtesy of Jessie Cohen, OGE, National Zoological Park, Smithsonian Institution, Washington, D.C.

Photos on pages 6, 16 (left), and 28 courtesy of Milwaukee County Zoo

Photos on page 8, 20, and 25 by Dave Holmes

Photo on page 7 (right) by Animals, Animals/L. T. Rhodes

Photo on page 11 (left) by Animals, Animals/Miriam Austerman

Photo on page 11 (right) by Animals, Animals/Charles Palek

Photo on page 14 (bottom) by Animals, Animals/Bradley Smith

Photo on page 24 by Earth Scenes/E. R. Degginger

Photo on page 9 by Arch McLean

Photos on pages 15, 17, 18 (center), and 29 (right) by David L. Denemark

Photos on page 10 and 16 (right) courtesy of Gladys Porter Zoo, Brownsville, Texas

Photos on page 12 by James P. Rowan

Photo on page 13 by Bill West, Carolina Biological Supply Co.

Photo on page 30 (bottom) by Guy LaBranche, Department of Wildlife and Fisheries, State of Louisiana, Baton Rouge

Library of Congress Cataloging-in-Publication Data

Tester, Sylvia Root
    A visit to the zoo.

    (Field trip series)
    Summary: A group of children sees many different kinds of animals while on a class trip to the zoo.
    1. Zoo animals—Juvenile literature.   2. Zoos—Juvenile literature.   [1. Zoo animals.   2. Zoos]
I. Title.   II. Series.
QL77.5.T47   1987   590'.74'4   84-12697
ISBN 0-516-01494-3

5 6 7 8 9 10 11 12 R 95 94 93 92

a visit to the ZOO

Created by The Child's World

Mrs. Block's class is at the zoo for a visit.

"The zoo is a big place," Mrs. Block says. "We want you to have fun. But we don't want you to get lost. So we will go in small groups. Please stay with your group."

Pam and Kay go with Mrs. Jones. So do
Steve, Bob, Mark, and Brian. Mrs. Jones is
Mark's mother. She is helping the teacher
on this trip. Mrs. Jones lets the children
choose where to go first. They vote for see-
ing the elephants.

The children walk down the path.
"Dana's group is already watching the
elephants," says Pam. "I think they walked
faster than we did."

Dana has a good place to stand and watch.

The rhinoceroses live nearby. So the
children stop next to see them. The rhinos
are busy eating. "They sure are funny
looking," Kay says. Everyone agrees.

A baby camel is eating too. The children
stop to watch. "I'm glad that most of the
animals are not in cages," says Brian.

Mama waits patiently while her baby
finishes breakfast.

The next stop is to see the big cats.

"These are my favorites," Kay says. "But
I don't know if I like tigers or lions best."

Two tigers are taking a sun bath.

"I wonder if tigers purr like my kittens?"
Steve asks. But the other children don't
know.

The lions seem to like their zoo home. Maybe it reminds them of their home in Africa.

The male lions are too lazy to care about the children who are watching them. But a lioness stares at the children from high up on a rock.

The children visit the reptile house next. They want to see the crocodiles and alligators.

"Look at this crocodile," Bob says. "It looks mean. See its teeth."

An alligator lays by the water. "I wish the alligator would move while we're here," Pam says. But it doesn't. No wonder some people think alligators look like logs.

The turtles live in the reptile house too.
"What a big turtle!" Pam says.
"Some turtles live in the water," Mrs.
Jones tells the children. "Other turtles live
on land. But some can live either place."
Soon the children start for the penguin
house.

On the way, they walk past a family of
swans. "Baby swans are called cygnets,"
Mrs. Jones tells them.

In the penguin house Bob says, "Waddle, waddle." He walks like a penguin.
Everyone laughs. Then they are off to see
the kangaroos.

The children try to decide what the kangaroos see. They are looking at something.

"Maybe they're looking at us," Kay says. "I wish one of them had a baby in its pocket."

Several of the giraffes are out for a walk. So the children walk over to where they can see one close-up.

"Giraffes are the tallest animals in the world," Mrs. Jones says. "And their patchy color makes them hard to see in the wild."

The zebras are nearby. So the children look at them next. One is standing almost close enough to pet. But nobody can reach it.

Pam thinks the zebra has black stripes. Steve says the stripes are white. What do you think?

A family is already looking at the sea
lions when the group gets there. Some of
the sea lions are sitting on a rock. But
others are swimming about.

Nearby, the children get to watch a zoo keeper feeding an otter.

"It is almost time for our lunch too," Mrs. Jones says. "So we must hurry along."

The children set off for the picnic grounds to find the rest of the class. But on the way they pass a hippopotamus. It is on its way into a pool.

Some people call hippos, *River Horses*. Hippos have short legs, thick skin, and almost no hair.

It's time for the children to eat their
sandwiches and cookies. They quickly sit
down at the tables. "It feels good to sit
down, doesn't it?" asks Mrs. Block. The
children agree.

"Later, we will see the dolphins eat their
lunch," Mrs. Block adds. "The show is at
two o'clock."

After lunch, the class visits the petting
zoo. Pam makes friends with the black and
white goats. So do Beth and Mike.

But Bob tries to decide if he really wants
to pet a snake.

Going to the dolphin show, the class passes the bears. "We still have time to look at them," Mrs. Jones says.

The big brown bears are walking around. Perhaps they have come out to enjoy the sunshine. Or maybe they are playing "parade," walking back and forth, back and forth.

One white polar bear has been for a
swim. The other thinks he might just climb
up on the rock and take a nap.

"Let's hurry," says Mrs. Jones. "We want
to be on time for the dolphin show."

The dolphins are already swimming about in the pool when the children take their seats for the show. As the show begins, the dolphins leap high in the air. Everyone claps. People cheer.

One dolphin jumps through a ring and
gets a fish for a reward. Quickly the other
comes up to see if it will get a fish too.
Watching the dolphins is fun.

After the show, Mrs. Jones and the children go to see the monkeys. First they stop to watch the monkeys on monkey island. Some jump. Others run about. But many of them just sit and stare back at the children.

Next the group goes to see the great apes. A young orangutan is so cute he makes the children giggle. But they don't giggle at the big, black gorilla. Would you?

Too soon it is time to leave. Mrs. Jones
and the children start for the bus. On the
way, they see a baby gazelle having an
afternoon snack and a mother deer look -
ing for her fawn.

"We didn't have time to see all the animals," Tommy says. The groups are gathering at the bus.

"We never do," a helper says.

"I'm going to ask my dad to bring me back," Tommy says. "The zoo is a great place to visit."